It's Time to Start Winning

SIMON CAPON

Contents

1. A New Direction in Thinking 1

2. My Story... 5

3. The Cycle of Success 13

4. State.. 18

5. Physiology 19

6. A Life Without Emotion...................................... 24

7. The Emotional Brain... 25

8. Programmes.. 31

9. A Simple Example.. 33

10. Language.. 35

11. Beliefs 40

12. Experiences... 47

13. Attitudes 52

14. Decisions... 58

15. Mental Rehearsal 62

16. Summary.. 68

17. Putting It All Together 69

18. The Solution.. 72

19. Stacey's Four-Step Strategy................................. 75

20. Additional Skills.. 76

21. Let's Speed Things Up 77

22. Instant Self-Belief 79

23. The Steps for Instant Self-Belief 84

24. The Rapid-Change Technique 86

25. The Steps for the Rapid-Change Technique 92

26. Goal Setting.. 95

27. Relaxed Body.. 100

28. Progressive Relaxation 101

29. The Red Mist 103

30. It's All Yours... 105

A New Direction in Thinking

It was a warm summer evening on the 16th of August 2009. Berlin was the host city for the IAAF World Championships in Athletics. The men's 100m final would be contested by the eight fastest people on the planet. All eyes, however, were on two athletes who were the dominant forces in sprinting: the then-reigning world champion from the USA, Tyson Gay; and the Olympic champion and world-record holder, Jamaica's Usain Bolt. The stadium was full, with an expectant crowd about to experience one of the greatest moments in sporting history.

As the athletes were being announced, Usain Bolt stood with a smile on his face. His posture was one of certainty. He seemed completely unfazed by the expectations of a global audience. There was a moment of complete silence in the packed stadium as Bolt settled himself.

The starter gun fired. Instantly, he shot out the blocks like a bullet. Forty strides later, at a speed of more than 40kph, Usain Bolt smashed his own world record and destroyed his world-class opposition. His time was an astonishing 9.58 seconds. He not only added a world title to his increasing collection of accolades, but produced a time that many thought was beyond human capability.

At the end of the race, he faced a barrage of questions from the media. One reporter asked, "Can you describe that race?" The great man smiled and replied, "I felt good, and I just executed it." He didn't talk about the pressure, the expectations of the crowd, or his rivalry with Tyson Gay. He simply spoke about his intention: to run his race to the best of his ability.

Usain Bolt is a man who many labelled superhuman. Although he has an exceptional talent, he is no more of a superhuman than you or me. However, he has created an incredible mindset that provides a laser focus on the task at hand, no matter the occasion or the location.

One of our greatest challenges is to accept that we can orchestrate our thoughts, behaviours and results by understanding and accepting that we are their creator. Most have concluded that our outside environment is solely responsible for our feelings. Many players, coaches and managers firmly place the blame on outside circumstances for their lack of self-belief and anxieties. Unfortunately, this is widely accepted by most athletes and teams. We are conditioned to assume that the events that occur around us are solely responsible for generating our emotions.

A tennis player invests substantial amounts of time and effort on her practise routines. The practise court is where she produces a consistency that is admired and envied by others. She has become familiar and comfortable with her ability to play and win competitions.

As she develops, she is invited to bigger events playing at exclusive venues. But now, the whole atmosphere seems very different: she now faces higher-quality opposition, and winning matches means payday. The sights and sounds seem to produce anxiety and frustration. People whom she has respect for confirm that these events will create nervous energy because they are more important, and prize money is available. She accepts this, and goes through her career with a belief that the outside events are to blame for her emotions. This occurs far too often; but the real tragedy is that it only requires a new direction in thinking to trigger a series of events that will put her in the driving seat of her perceptions, feelings and behaviours.

Through this book, my purpose is for you to accept complete responsibility for your thoughts, emotions and actions. When you look at the environment and external factors for your chances of success or failure, you are amongst the majority. Most live in hope that they will feel energised and focused when it matters the most, and have concluded that they have little or no control over these factors. When you take full accountability for the way you feel, you automatically move from the effect to its cause.

This book is much more than just a manual for sport. It's a manual that will affect you in every aspect of your life. We all have challenges, some more than others; and perhaps you are experiencing circumstances that may seem overwhelming. But with a different mindset, you can become the master of your own destiny.

Most will read this book once and place it on a shelf to gather dust. The major reason this happens is simple. The majority confuse information with knowledge. Allow me to explain. Let's assume you are visiting a town you are unfamiliar with. I ask you to meet me at the library. I have written the instructions, which read like this:

1. As you come out of the train station, cross the road and take the second left, followed by an immediate right.

2. Carry on walking a further 100 metres, where you will see the entrance to a shopping centre.

3. Walk through the centre to the exit, and through the automatic doors.

4. From here, you will see the library in front of you.

When you repeat this process several times, you won't need the written instructions; you will find your way to the library without much conscious effort. The information has now become knowledge. When knowledge is coupled with massive action, virtually anything is possible.

A good friend who seemed to have a wealth of knowledge on a wide range of topics advised me to stop reading eight books once; but instead, read one book eight times. I urge you to follow his example, be the exception, and read this book multiple times so it becomes your guide and partner in becoming the best version of yourself. You now have the opportunity to accomplish what very few people attain: fulfilling your true potential.

My Story

My personal fascination with the mind (or more specifically, the mindset) within sports began when I was 16 years of age. During the '80s, the British government introduced the Youth Training Scheme or Y.T.S. It was designed to help school-leavers develop and learn a trade of their choice.

While others were learning how to fix engines, build houses and tile floors, I was the first person in the UK to be given the opportunity to join the Y.T.S. and study the art of snooker. The club where I played gave me a key to the building so I could practise whenever I wished.

Most mornings, at 7 am, I would set up my practise routine. I was alone and loved every second. Unfortunately, something would happen a couple of hours later that changed everything. At 10 am, the club opened, and people came in. There was nothing extraordinary about this. However, when I was observed, or I played an opponent, it was as if my personality changed. I had a huge fear of failure, and a greater fear of other people's expectations. The point of practice is to win tournaments. Unfortunately, due to my anxieties, this didn't happen as often as it should.

It soon became public knowledge that I had been accepted for a year on the Y.T.S., and the snooker club understandably wanted as much publicity as possible. Within a few days, I was on the local ITV channel, and I appeared in the *Daily Mirror* newspaper and the front page of our local paper. As a result, my fear of failure was growing, and my fear of other people's expectations was getting out of control. I kept this a secret; it seemed unrealistic that other players would understand.

The only person whom I trusted with this was my coach. One afternoon, he asked me for my thoughts. I explained that I felt so much pressure. He looked at me and said, "Pressure? What pressure?"

I replied, "The pressure of my fear of failure; but most of all, the fear of what other people think of me as a player."

He paused for a moment and said, "That's interesting because when you practise alone, or you play competitively, you are physically the same person, your cue is the same, the table is the same, and so are the balls." He then looked straight into my eyes. "You have created this, and I can't help you. You will have to sort this out yourself." He then stood up and walked away, leaving me with frustrated, angry and very confused thoughts. I decided I would just get on with it. Perhaps I would grow out of it? The reality was that over the coming weeks, months and years, it progressively got worse.

It was the first round of the UK championship. I was drawn to play an Australian opponent. The day before my match, I wandered through a corridor of the hotel and overheard a conversation with two players. One said to the other, "Have you seen the Australian guy? He is worse than useless; I've no idea why he even bothered turning up." Upon hearing this, my fear of failure was now at its peak; my fear of others' expectations was through the roof.

I went into that match terrified. Without a doubt, it was one of the worst performances I've ever experienced. Before I knew it, I was 3-0 down. I lost the match 5-0. As I walked out of the playing area, I labelled myself as someone who couldn't hold his nerve, had no courage, and possessed absolutely no bottle whatsoever. I placed my cue back into the case, and never played a competitive match again.

Fifteen years later, I was in my kitchen, cooking. The television was on for nothing more than background noise when the presenter mentioned N.L.P. I asked myself, "What's that?" I went over to my laptop and typed it into the search box. The result came up with neuro-linguistic programming, a relatively new science and psychology. But the more I read, the more intense my enthusiasm became. It was one of those lightbulb moments. I clearly remember thinking to myself, "This is what I've been looking for during the last twenty years."

I signed up instantly for a practitioner course. I studied every hour possible, then travelled to London for the intensive training program. Every coffee break, at lunchtimes and during the evenings, I would ask the trainers question after question.

After a couple of days, one of the trainers took me to one side, smiled and said, "Thank you for bringing so much enthusiasm to the training. I'm going to explain something that I think will be extremely helpful to you. This is basically how it all works. Whenever you receive any information from one or more of your five senses, you create a meaning. In other words, you see, hear, feel, smell or taste something. You decide if it's good, bad, happy, sad or anything in between. The meaning you create becomes your reality. Your reality will generate an emotion. This triggers an action or behaviour which will produce a result. So instead of trying to change the result, focus on changing the meaning which becomes your new reality, and the rest will follow."

To this day, this was one of the most important conversations I have ever had. I thought about my coach's words all those years ago. He was right all along. It occurred to me that I was the only problem I had, and I was the only solution.

I completed the intensive training program, passed my exam, and went home to study. I read every book, downloaded every course, and attended all the seminars I could. I became a master practitioner and trainer of N.L.P.; and brought together many psychological skills to produce a model that, with practice, will change your life forever.

Because of this model, I have worked with GB athletes (both able-bodied and disabled), English and Scottish international athletes, professional footballers, golfers, tennis players, and two world champions. I have written for *Tennis Life Magazine,* I am currently a columnist for *UK Tennis Magazine,* and I made an appearance in the BBC documentary *Race for Rio.*

We are all designed to make our mark. I once imagined that I would make mine on the green baize, but it was never to become reality. Looking back, I certainly lacked the ability to perform anywhere near the level required. But because of my experiences, I understand some of the difficulties faced by competitors. Life constantly delivers opportunities, and I'm hugely grateful that I'm able to put my past experiences and challenges to good use. I'm committed to helping as many people as possible to become certain that whatever their circumstances, they have everything they need to accept any challenge full in the face and enjoy the experience. Anxiety is partly due to uncertainty. When you have true self-belief in your ability to remain focused in any situation, you become a very different competitor than the one you used to be.

Understanding my story, I'm sure you can appreciate my frustration when I hear the opinion of some that many sportspeople lack bottle. This mostly comes from an overdramatic media that spends so much time, energy and effort looking for examples wherein a perceived pressure situation become too much for the competitor, and they simply didn't fulfil their expectations. This scenario is common; and has a ripple effect when our national teams appear in world cups, Olympic Games, and other high-profile global events. You will hear conversations at bus stops, public transport and bars all over the country where people who confess to zero knowledge suddenly became experts after watching a five-minute report by a journalist paid to paint a dull and hopeless picture of our national teams' chances of success. Within the pages of this book, I am going to paint a very different picture for you. It's not one of hope, but one of certainty that every one of us already has everything we need to design and produce the ultimate competitive mindset.

We all listen to interviews from managers and coaches, but perhaps I listen to them with very different ears. A Premier League football manager explained that his team had suffered three successive defeats; and what they now required was, in his words, "A bit of luck, and a win to inject [his] team with some confidence." What he is saying is that something external must happen (a bit of luck, and a different result) to produce an internal emotion which, in this case, is confidence. The reality is that anyone can have any emotion they choose instantly. They don't have to wait for an event or situation to occur; we all have everything to instigate an emotion immediately.

Allow me to demonstrate. I want you to think of a specific time you experienced one of the following: an event wherein you felt extremely happy and proud, or an occasion where you found something very amusing. Take some time to remember then relive a moment when you either won a tournament, ran a personal-best time, or scored the winning goal. Perhaps you committed to a tough training program; maybe you watched a loved one put every ounce of energy into an important event. Or you could have a memory of someone telling a joke, having a night out when you didn't stop laughing, or watched a video on YouTube. Whatever it is, make sure the memory is one that fills you with a positive emotion.

Once you have chosen a memorable event, relive it now by closing your eyes and allowing yourself to go back to that specific time. See the event through your own eyes. Make the images big, bright and colourful; and the sounds loud. Notice the emotions returning. Don't rush anything; simply allow the positive feelings to generate organically.

If you find this difficult, I'm sure you have experienced a time when you were going about your day when you suddenly remembered a joke or something amusing a friend shared with you. You instantly started laughing. This is an example of you creating an emotion that wasn't produced by an external stimulus. You were the creator of your thought and feelings. I understand that for a lasting change, it's going to take more; but it does demonstrate that you are in control, or at least more in control than you perhaps imagined.

We have all been gifted with the most sophisticated and powerful bio-computer, which is, of course, the human brain. We use it for every thought, feeling and action without ever contemplating if we could use it to a greater potential. It's comfortable to conclude that we have little say in our thoughts and emotions. Unfortunately, it's also common for people over the age of forty to decide they cannot change. You will hear on many occasions that if they could change their mindset, they would have done it years ago. They have given up on their dreams, and allowed mediocrity to settle in. The desire to achieve their big goals has given way to a more comfortable way of thinking. Sadly, this thinking pattern is one that seems to influence much younger competitors as well. The outcome of this poor thinking means you will never accomplish your full potential. However, you are now at the beginning of a greater understanding of your mind, and how you can make long-term changes. These changes include your self-belief, confidence and courage; and can be implemented no matter how old you are.

Professional sport invests huge sums on the physical and technical aspects. But far too often, only a fraction is devoted to the importance of a strong mind. This answers the question of why so many talented sportswomen and men who perform at such high levels in a training environment show little of this when competing in big events. The value of a greater understanding with strategies to develop a fitter and more productive mind is key to becoming the best version of yourself.

Having a focused mind is a skill that requires effort and practice. Going to the gym to work out, running on the track under floodlights when it's cold and raining, or swimming countless lengths are all investments in your sport. Taking time to produce a much stronger mindset is also an investment that most are not prepared to pay. Be different and make space in your schedule to learn, act and master the greatest skill of all: the ability to master your mind. Decide now that you will take massive action and commit to becoming the very best version of yourself.

Let's begin.

The Cycle of Success

Whenever I meet a new student, they always want me to assist them in obtaining a better result. When you think about it, that's what we all want. We all want to experience success, and we also feel that we are judged by our results.

From an early age, we watch the sporting greats win the biggest prizes on offer. Their successes are the talk in every school, workplace and social gathering. We dream about replicating their triumphs; and imagine how it must feel to have the masses watching us in awe, and with complete admiration.

So, the plan is to achieve greatness by winning matches and tournaments with monotonous regularity, and moving up the ladder with speed. However, it's very unlikely to happen. Even the sporting gods had to endure tough times, which included many painful defeats. The result of our planning for fast success is a mindset that suggests a seamless succession of tournament wins is essential.

By implementing this approach, we instinctively focus on the result and nothing else. When our awareness is solely on the result, it's easy to become aware, concerned and fearful of the possibility of failure. We naturally avoid failure (for a reason I will explain later), along with a strong resistance to being regarded as a failure by others. I'm sure you have experienced anxiety that was promoted by the apprehension of a bad result. It's important to understand that these are natural ways of thinking.

My purpose is to take your thinking to a new direction wherein you will find much less resistance. If the result is producing nerves and anxiety, where do you need to place your attention? This simple diagram helps direct your focus to the components that lead to a better result whilst retaining your focus on performance.

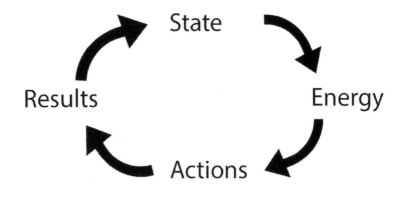

This is a simple yet extremely effective way of looking at any competitive-sport scenario, or any test, for that matter. Everyone wants a great result, but you must first go back a few steps. Look at the diagram and allow me to explain.

Let's start at the top, where it says 'state'. If you have a negative or poor state, it's unlikely that you will tap fully into your energy reservoir. This will have an impact on your actions, which are likely to be tentative and uncertain. Performing these actions will likely produce a poor result, which reinforces your original poor state.

Let's look at the opposite scenario. You have a mindset which includes self-belief and confidence coupled with a feeling of assertiveness. These are, of course, very important components that produce the ultimate state. You are ready to invest every ounce of effort into your performance. This new state means you will produce an abundance of energy with enthusiasm and focus. This automatically produces assertive actions, and you will likely receive a far greater result. This, of course, reinforces your original positive state.

At this point, it's easy to assume you have four components to focus on, but the reality is that you only need to focus on two. If you take care of your state and actions, your energy and results will take care of themselves. To look at this in more detail, look at these two scenarios. Both people we will focus on have very similar aspirations to not only compete, but to push themselves to the limit and enjoy a favourable result. The difference is how they set themselves up to achieve their goals and ambitions.

Jeanette is an accomplished half-marathon runner. She has travelled the world competing, and has a very respectable PB of 1 hour and 40 minutes. Jeanette is highly competitive, and couldn't resist the opportunity to take up mountain biking. She joins a club and instantly signs up for a 10k challenge. Even though she is new to the sport, her competitive instincts awaken, and she sets a target to complete the distance in two hours. Even though experienced riders suggest that this is possibly a little ambitious, she sticks to her plan. As the day of the race edges closer, her thoughts are on the result, which is the two-hour completion time she set for herself. Although off-road cycling is new to her, Jeanette is not one to set targets only to fail.

The day of the ride arrives. As she prepares and makes her way to the start line, she is in a state of apprehension. She feels her energy levels lowering by the minute. As she begins the ride, her lack of energy has a huge impact on her physical ability to push hard (her 'Actions'). This continues around the course, which explains why she came in with a time of 2 hours and 30 minutes. This is still a respectable time for a beginner, but certainly not the result she wanted. This perceived poor result then reinforces her state of apprehension and lack of belief regarding her ability to perform at the level she expects. By putting all her attention on the result, she begins a chain reaction. By understanding this, a new strategy to calm her thoughts and emotions is required.

Another rider who is equally inexperienced has a very different mindset. Beth is the same age as Jeanette, and shares a very competitive attitude. She plays several sports, including tennis and squash at county level, so she has also experienced sporting success.

Like Jeanette, Beth also gives herself a target time that would test her. However, she directs her focus to her state. She feels excited and extremely enthusiastic at the start line. Her positive state generates huge volumes of energy that fuels a powerful physical performance. During the ride, she is able to place her attention on the technical aspects of off-road cycling that she had learnt from more experienced competitors ('Actions'). This produces a great result, which predictably refuels her excited state.

These two events illustrate the importance of targeting your attention to state and actions. Your actions are what you learn from coaches, trainers and manuals. They are the physical, technical and strategic aspects of your chosen sport. It's what you learn on the practise field. Clearly, the first piece of the model is state. But what is state; and how can you design, produce and use it to your advantage?

State

I'm sure you are familiar with the phrase "a state of mind". You can experience a good or bad state. You may experience a resourceful or negative state. A state is basically how you feel about yourself and your abilities at any given moment. This directly affects how you perceive any situation. When you're in a great state, you can feel that you are unstoppable. However, when you encounter a poor state, virtually anything can be a problem.

You will tend to move from one to the other and anything in between during your day, so first we must understand what a state is and how it's produced. A state is made up of two components: physiology and internal representations (what's going on in our minds). So, let's start with physiology.

Physiology

The way you sit, walk, stand or even breathe affects your state. Have you ever noticed someone on the street, someone you didn't know and who hadn't spoken a word to you, but you instinctively knew they were in a state of confidence? This happens all the time, and it's called intuition. Think about Usain Bolt, Michael Phelps, Roger Federer or Serena Williams. All have achieved extraordinary levels of success. Whenever they compete, they carry a magnitude of expectations. Watch any video of them before a grand slam or Olympic final, and take notice of their physiology. Believe me, they are not immune to nerves, but they understand their ability to implement confidence and certainty.

The reality is that there is a science behind it. You can learn how to produce confidence with a better posture, and it takes seconds. If you'll take one skill from this book, then this is it. Confidence is not a gift given to the elite. Confidence is a state of mind that anyone can learn and master, and it starts with physiology. Let's begin with a demonstration:

1. Think of someone whom you would rather not spend time with, someone whom you have a negative response to. When you see this person, you automatically walk in the opposite direction

to avoid them. Notice how you create a negative internal feeling when you think of them.

2. Now take your thoughts to something neutral, i.e., the weather or the time; or look around the room. This book was never designed to create a negative effect, so shake it off quickly.

3. Stand up tall and proud, with your shoulders back and head held high, and smile. Then exaggerate this posture. Stand on your tiptoes, look up at the ceiling, and smile the biggest and cheesiest grin you can muster up. (You only need to exaggerate this for the first few practice attempts.)

4. Now remain in this extreme posture, and bring back the image of the person you thought of when you created that negative feeling.

5. Notice that although you can bring back the image, there is no negative response. If there is, then you simply need to stretch up taller, or smile bigger and brighter.

6. By creating this posture, you are taking the first steps in generating a positive state. Consistency will produce confidence and certainty.

Now, I'm not suggesting you walk around staring at the stars on tiptoes with a silly grin on your face. After all, questions will be asked regarding your sanity. But the exercise gives you a better understanding of your physiology. When you take on a posture of confidence and certainty, your mind accepts this to be true and creates an emotion that mirrors it.

For fun, take on a weak and uncertain posture. Sit down, lean forward, and allow your body to slump. Internally voice some positive words. Say to yourself, "I'm feeling fired-up today. I will set the world alight." Attempt to use a commanding tone, and try to create excitement. Notice how difficult it is? In fact, it feels so unnatural, you will find it challenging to remain in that physical position.

The first task is to adopt your new physiology. Make a conscious decision that you will check it during the day. In fact, whenever you feel any negative emotions, reposition yourself immediately. Stand tall with your shoulders back and head held high. Whilst maintaining this posture, take slow and deep breaths for two minutes. In as little as two minutes, your state will change significantly.

My suggestion to you is that you practise this short exercise every morning, before you step outside and begin your day. Just a couple of minutes will make sure you are ready to attack the day self-assured and with bags of energy. From here on, ensure that you stand, walk and move with your head held high, back straight, and shoulders back. Make every gesture, every step one of stability and purpose.

I went through a short period of time wherein I felt focused and extremely confident for a few days, only to experience self-doubt and apprehension. I attended a family party, and the moment was captured with many pictures and videos. When I looked at some of the photos, I was taken back when I noticed my poor posture.

I mentioned this to a group of colleagues. One said, "Every ninety minutes."

I asked, "Every ninety minutes?"

He replied, "You must check your physiology every ninety minutes."

Now I would be stretching the truth if I said I checked it that often. However, I did implement the two-minute exercise every morning, and checked it whenever I felt my state slip. It was an invaluable lesson, and one I will never underestimate.

By implementing physiology of confidence, you will automatically produce greater quantities of energy. We all have days when we struggle to feel motivated or inspired to go out and train. When you hear the rain hitting your bedroom window coupled with a strong wind, it's likely you will feel the energy being drained from your body. A strong physiology promotes higher energy levels that are crucial for a long-term training program.

I suggest you evaluate your levels of energy with a mark between 1 and 10. 1, you're sleepwalking; 10, you're unstoppable. Become consciously aware of your levels before you begin training. It's desirable to be at a 9 or a 10. If you were to make sure that every day, you never let your energy fall any lower than an 8, imagine how much more productive training sessions would become?

When you have great physiology and an abundance of energy, envisage how your performances will change along with your results. To begin with, put all your efforts into practising this until it becomes an unconscious habit. Be mindful of how you feel when you consistently retain a great posture. Notice the comments you receive from other people. Don't be surprised when they notice you are more confident and self-assured. They probably won't be able to pinpoint what is different, but you will. Get ready to enjoy just one of your secret weapons.

A Life Without Emotion

Who would you be without emotion? Take a moment to imagine a life without psychological feelings. How would you experience life's challenges?

On the face of it, this sounds very appealing when you cast your memory back to events where negative emotions have held you back; prevented you from performing at your best; and, in some cases, even prevented you from performing at all. Before you wish you could live such a life, remember that excitement, joy, confidence, love and happiness are also emotions. Living life without all of these would be extremely dull and prevent the intention of your very existence, which is to grab life by the horns and go for it! Take every opportunity, learn from every experience, and live every moment.

The emotions you experience can take you to the heights of exhilaration or the depths of despair. Up until now, you have almost certainly been at the mercy of your emotional thinking. From this point forward, you will have the knowledge and ability to handle these once-uncontrollable feelings. To begin the journey, you must first understand where they come from.

The Emotional Brain

It's the Wimbledon ladies' final. The competitors have entered Centre Court, and begin their pre-match rituals. Both players have shown their ability to compete at the very highest level, and earn their place in the history books through one of the sport's greatest events.

Observing these remarkable athletes, it's easy to watch in admiration and conclude that they somehow are immune to the negative emotions that mere mortals suffer. The fact is that like us, they are human; and although we are all unique, we all have a brain. However, there is a part of our brain that operates only with emotions, both positive and negative. To make this easy to understand, we will call this part the 'emotional brain'. The elite athlete has mastered the ability to remain focused and decisive in almost any situation. They have learnt how to manage their emotional brain and even use it to their advantage. So, what is it?

When our prehistoric ancestors were living in a primitive world, they were faced with the real possibility that at any moment, they could be attacked by a predator. This would likely happen when least expected. So for the survival of the species, their brain had to not only respond, but have the capability to instantly direct their full focus, energy and attention to a survival response. We now call this our 'fight, flight or freeze' response. When our primitive forebearers were faced with the strong possibility that they were going to be lunch for a hunter, they would call upon one of these instincts. Fight, and they will stand up to the attacker. Flight, and they run for their lives; or freeze in the hope that they won't be noticed. The response is simply to survive and remain safe.

Because their lives depended on this fight, flight or freeze response, the body would borrow energy from other parts to maximise their chances of success, and enabling extra energy to be pumped into the legs and upper body to produce greater speed and agility. This was extremely effective when we were living in such primitive surroundings. However, our environment is, thankfully, much safer and civilised. We are unlikely to encounter such an experience, but we are still preloaded with the same fight, flight or freeze response.

This is just one aspect of the emotional brain. Although you are not threatened in the same way, your emotional brain's development in comparison to the other parts of the brain has been very slow. It still has a duty to keep you safe and alive, so it will look for any potential problems. To ensure that you consciously take notice, it will perceive a situation to be much bigger than it really is.

For example, Ben is travelling to a competition. The traffic is more congested than normal. He looks at his watch: he only has forty-five minutes before his first-round match. But according to the GPS, he still has ten miles to travel. His pre-match routine allows him twenty minutes to warm up and settle himself, but it's likely he will have to abandon this and start the match immediately. He becomes anxious and vocal, shouting at the traffic in a vain attempt to make it move like a frightened herd of cattle.

Looking at this scenario logically, it seems that Ben is getting stressed without reason. He is likely to make it to the competition, and will only suffer a little knock in his startup routine. What happened was his emotional brain put a spotlight on the situation in an attempt to make this small issue a much bigger problem. By doing this, Ben now creates urgency, and will do anything to ensure he finds a solution.

This happens to us during our everyday lives. When a small issue seems to be growing into a big problem, stop and appreciate that your emotional brain is distorting the situation by putting a spotlight on it to make you take immediate action.

Another of the emotional brain's prime directives is to avoid failure at all cost. It believes that failure could be fatal. Again, going back to a primitive age, our ancestors had to hunt to survive. Fail to land a successful hunt, and they may starve.

Have you ever taken an exam, completed the paper, and felt very confident that you will achieve a high mark? You won't receive the results for many weeks, so you feel relaxed and happy that you have passed. As the day of the results gets closer, you feel slight anxiety, which gradually increases up to the big day. Even though you felt extremely confident at the end of the exam, you now experience apprehension and the dreaded fear of failure.

This happens to many students, and is a result of thinking naturally. Your emotional brain is trying to take away the possibility of failure by creating an emotion that becomes so strong, you would put off opening the envelope or email. This way, you never know if you have failed; and more importantly, others won't either.

Which brings us nicely to the emotional brain's third prime directive.

The emotional brain feels you need to be part of a group. This provides safety in numbers. Once again, it has an unrealistic belief that if you are left alone, you are unprotected and easy picking for predators. Of course, we all know that this is nonsense. But to your emotional brain, this is a reality. It's there to protect you, and it will at all cost.

Imagine that you are preparing to play the first 18 holes of the county golf championship. You step out of the clubhouse and make your way to the first tee. As you approach, you can see a small gathering of spectators and other competitors. You are consciously aware that you have played this initial shot on countless occasions. You had executed this shot without thought, but this is different. This time, it matters: there is an expectation from yourself and others.

As you approach the shot, your emotions seem to take over; and you feel you have little or no control. Your inner voice begins to question your ability to play this shot under so much pressure. Your focus automatically moves to the strong possibility that the ball could go anywhere. "What if I slice it? What if I scuff it?" Now all you want to do is get it out of the way and move away from the critical eyes of the spectators. In fact, if you could, you would pass on this shot altogether.

So, what's going on? Remember, your emotional brain demands you be a part of a group to remain safe. As you play the shot in front of an expectant crowd, your emotional brain is saying something like this: "If you get this wrong, they will think you're a rank amateur. They may even laugh out loud, and feel embarrassed that they are even watching you. Perhaps they may talk about you to others, who will spread the word that you're an extremely poor competitor who can't be taken seriously."

How many times have you felt the stress of being watched when competing? This is far too common and, on many occasions, players from all sports have come to the false conclusion that they lack bottle to compete under such conditions.

This is in no way exclusive to expectant spectators. Remember, the emotional brain is programmed to avoid failure. If it feels you are putting yourself forward in a situation where failure is a strong possibility, it will protest in the hope that you will give in and return to a safe, non-competitive environment where you can survive in the contentment of your comfort zone. Knowledge is important, but knowledge with the ability to change perceptions coupled with action is extremely powerful.

We all possess an emotional brain. We can't get rid of it; but with a better understanding, we can learn to work with it. In later chapters, I will explain how to use its huge energy and direct it so you produce courage, confidence and certainty in such volumes that you will become an unstoppable force; and it all happens in just a few seconds. It's incredible, and the results can be life-changing.

Programmes

Now that you have a better understanding of the emotional brain, we should look at how this all works. Perhaps in an ideal world, you would accept information from one or more of your five senses, create meaning, and behave in a very calm and calculated manner. The reality is that the emotional brain will attach any emotion it feels necessary to any situation. This could be a positive emotion like excitement or joy; or it may generate a negative emotion, for example, anxiety and fear. This happens so you take immediate action to ensure you are kept safe.

However, there is another aspect that is perhaps the most important: programmes. It's important to understand that our programmes are metaphorical, but they do provide us with a workable model that makes it easy to understand and implement change. We all have the same programmes, but the information stored in them is vastly different for everyone. These programmes are language, beliefs, decisions, experiences and attitudes. These programmes create what we call in N.L.P. an association; but for simplicity, we will see them as a guide to the emotional brain, which will behave how it feels necessary with the information the programmes have offered.

The diagram below explains how this process works.

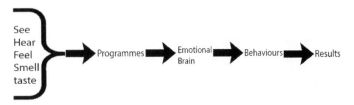

We receive information through one or more of our five senses. This raw information is fed to the programmes. The programmes contain information that's been loaded during our lives. The data stored in the programmes are fed to the emotional brain that will respond by producing an emotion that's in line with the information it has received. This emotion will likely trigger a behaviour, which produces a result. The loading of data to the programmes happens whenever we apply meaning to any experience or result. Fortunately, it can be changed with intent. Over time, this change will feed new information to the emotional brain, which will respond in a significantly different way.

A Simple Example

Tom is a 400m hurdler. He has a new coach who understands his potential, but has changed his stride pattern to increase his pace between hurdles. For the last two years, Tom has enjoyed a great deal of success with his old pattern, but understands that changes must be made if he is to become a better athlete.

He trains hard but struggles with the new technique. He enters his first competitive race. Between hurdle three and four, his stride pattern breaks down; and he finishes a very disappointing third with a substandard time. This scenario continues for the next two races: each time, he misjudges the pattern early in the race. He feels frustrated and his confidence is declining. He runs possibilities over in his mind of continual setbacks and unacceptable times.

Although the poor results are certainly upsetting, it's what's happening at an unconscious level that is most important. His programmes are collecting information based on his judgments that suggest he is unable to run with this new technical change; which implies he will continue to perform badly and experience failure, disappointment and misery. Whenever he prepares for a competitive race, his emotional brain will receive information from the programmes that provide guidance with regard to the event. The programmes' data suggests a strong possibility of failure and despair. The emotional brain will react by filling his mind with anxiety, nerves, and even physical sickness if necessary. In fact, it will do whatever it needs to prevent him from competing and failing.

The good news is that we can reload the individual programmes, and it's much easier than you may think. We can begin with language.

Language

During a conversation with a student, I opened our meeting by saying, "Throughout our work together, I have one golden rule, which is to ban a simple word. That word is try." I explained that instead of "try", we'll simply say "just do it".

He looked at me, grinned and said, "I don't think it makes any difference."

I knew he had to be up early the following morning to catch the 6 am ferry from the Isle of Wight to Southampton. To redirect his thinking, I invited him to ask me if I could give him a lift to the ferry terminal at 5.30 am. He looked slightly puzzled, then asked if I could drive him to the terminal at 5.30 am. I paused and replied, "Ok, I will try my very hardest."

I asked him how confident he was that I will be there. He grinned and said, "I'm not sure if you will."

I then asked him to repeat the question. This time, my reply was "Absolutely, I will just do it."

At that moment, he began to understand the importance of our words. We generally use language unconsciously. In other words, we don't think about every word we say and, more importantly, the impact those words have.

To make sense of a sentence, you unconsciously create pictures, sounds or feelings. If I say Wimbledon, Olympics, World Cup, the US Open or Super Bowl, you will automatically generate a picture or movie in your mind. Your image may include sounds and feelings. Our use of language has a profound effect on the input of all the other programmes. The words you use to describe a belief, experience or decision will have an impact on how it appears in the programme.

For example, you are competing for your cricket team. You're the last man, and you need four runs to win on the last ball. As the ball is bowled, you instinctively go all out for the six. You connect perfectly, but the ball seems to remain in the air for a lifetime. It suddenly returns to earth and the eagle-eyed fielder catches it. You're out, and the team's fate is settled.

You watch in disbelief. You are stunned and empty; your inner voice screams at you: "Why did you play it that way? Everyone is looking at you, and you have let them all down. You just had to play the four, no heroics. Now you have to face the music, you idiot!" These words conjure up pictures, sounds and feelings of total misery. You're likely to have a belief that you have lost the match for your team and the experience is a complete failure.

A different way to use words to describe this could be: "I showed huge courage and went for it. I never hold back; I always give everything I have; and most of all, I have learnt that I stand up to a challenge with guts!" The use of language here will certainly load the data into the other programmes very differently, with a view of positivity and self-assurance.

Understand that the words you use to describe any experience will have a long-term effect, so choose them carefully. You will find it difficult to halt this, especially in the beginning. But with practice, you can and will do it.

When you find yourself consciously aware when you're using words of negativity, you're already making significant progress. Stick with this, and the long-term results will produce a calmer attitude and clearer thinking when you need it the most. The skill of using words will also have a profound effect on your current and long-term situation. You may understand that the words we use do not describe our reality of the world. They create it. Let's look at a scenario that many amateur runners will encounter.

You're a few weeks into a training program to run a marathon. The alarm goes off, so you pull off the warm duvet. Semi-consciously walk to the window and pull the curtains open. Only last night, the reliable weather girl said with unwavering confidence that you will be greeted with a partly cloudy morning, with no rain and very light winds. In short, it's perfect running weather.

But the scene outside is a very different story. The dark clouds are thickening, the wind is increasing dramatically, and it's beginning to rain heavily. You shake your head in disbelief; put your hands to your face; and say to yourself, "This is awful. I can't run in this. There is no way I'll be able to battle my way against this strong wind. The rain will be driving into my face, and I feel tired already." You then look at your inviting warm bed.

Before you know it, you're making a deal with yourself and saying, "Tomorrow, I will make up for it and run a little further than scheduled." Within a few minutes, you are back in the warm, cosy arena of blissful dreams.

The words you say to yourself will generate stories and pictures in your mind that drive you toward or away from what you need to do. A better analysis would be to look out the window and say to yourself, "Race day could bring unforgiving weather conditions. This gives me the perfect opportunity to train for the unexpected. Come on, give me your worst; you'll only make me stronger!" This provides a very different reaction, and conjures up a forceful, non-negotiable attitude.

But there is a very important aspect that is often overlooked: the tone of the inner voice. Notice the tone you have when you're making excuses or backing away from a challenge. It's likely to be timid and soft; you're never going to achieve much with the tones of hesitation and caution.

So, let me introduce to you your new coach. This coach is your new inner voice who only talks with certainty, confidence and overwhelming self-belief. He is the sergeant major. He will become your best and most loyal friend. He will never allow you to wallow in self-pity. Instead, he will metaphorically grab you by the hand, pull you up, and demand that you get back out there, take all the learning, and drive forward. He does this with a tone of authority and certainty.

Imagine what your sergeant major looks like. He will stand tall, proud shoulders held back, with his head held high. His voice will be strong, completely non-negotiable, and very straight-talking. He never feeds you with any negative dialogue. He always looks for new ideas and ways you can improve. He only uses words that take you forward. From today onward, your sergeant major will be with you every hour of every day. Say goodbye to all your excuses and reasons for why you didn't do all the things you know you need to. This is the new you, and you have the mentor to push you all the way.

Your sergeant major is strong, calm, controlled and certain. The tone of your sergeant major is crucial. When we finish a sentence, our tone either heightens, remains flat, or lowers. When we finish a sentence with a tone that heightens, we are asking a question. When the tone finishes flat, it's a statement. And when we lower the tone, it becomes a command. To create a tone of certainty, it must be a command. Whenever your sergeant major is active, his sentences must end with a lower tone, a command, a tone of certainty, as this diagram explains.

Techniques used: Better use of words, and 'sergeant major' inner voice.

Beliefs

Beliefs are essentially what we believe we can and cannot do. Beliefs are made up over time, and create our reality of what we think is achievable.

Let's say you are brought up in an environment full of people who have decided that fulfilling their dreams and ambitions simply isn't worth the effort. Perhaps they have suffered many disappointments, or they found that surviving within their comfort zone was adequate. Whatever their past, they have suffocated their desire to achieve their big goals.

But now their ego wants to make sure others don't accomplish theirs. If they did, it would only highlight their own failings. To prevent this, they will list the difficulties in detail that will persuade and prevent others from achieving anything that's above-average. After all, one of the emotional brain's prime directives is to be accepted by the group, and not seen as someone who is unsuccessful.

When someone is surrounded by sceptics and dream-stealers who have formed a habit of negative focus, there is a strong possibility that he or she will, in time, produce a belief that they are nothing more than another competitor. They will believe they are someone who should have realistic expectations and shouldn't fool themselves that they will achieve anything more than average or, at best, a respectable standard.

This happens every hour of every day, and talent is being lost. If you are at the opposite end of the spectrum, spending time with solution-focused individuals and groups who constantly look for positive meanings and outcomes, it's easy to understand how important this is and how it will have a significant effect on your beliefs.

Have you ever noticed how close friends, colleagues and family members often have the same mannerisms? They may share similar values and outlooks on life and its potential. We have already looked at how people we share time with can have an impact on our lives at a deep, unconscious level. They affect us in a way that consciously, we are rarely aware of.

An amateur tennis player I worked with understood the importance of this. He worked in an office with people he described as "soul-destroying". He asked me in desperation, "Do I need to get another job? My colleagues constantly focus on the difficulty of any task, and seem to enjoy the distress felt by other employees." He was in fear that he may slowly adopt the mindset of his co-workers. He was desperate to spend quality time with quality people, which seemed unrealistic in his current circumstances.

I asked him if he had access to the internet. He replied yes, of course. I asked him if he could spend time with anyone during lunchtime, and whom would it be. He went through a series of great tennis players, one of which was

Roger Federer. He smiled and said, "Yes, it's got to be Roger Federer. For me, he is the greatest of the greats."

I gave him a new routine that looked like this. He would find a space at work that no one occupied, and put on his headphones. I tasked him to spend his entire lunch hour watching his idol play and listening to him talking before and after a match, noticing his words and watching his physiology. The task was to immerse himself in the world of Roger Federer. He would then have the luxury of spending at least one hour a day with the great man. If possible, he would add another hour before he went to bed.

In the same way, as we unconsciously model our parents or people we spend a lot of time with, he was now thinking more like a confident, focused tennis player; he was thinking more like Roger Federer. This had a profound effect not only on his game, but on his personality. He was thinking differently, behaving differently and over time, producing much better results. He was changing his belief about who he was and what he could achieve. Like so many of these skills, it's incredibly simple; but simple ideas produce the biggest change.

Gregg was a basketball player who showed a raw talent. He was attracting a lot of interest from other teams, but enjoyed playing for his club. His main reason for remaining with his current squad was his huge respect for the coach. As far as Gregg was concerned, his mentor had experience and knowledge that was unrivalled.

During the season, Gregg suffered a loss of form, his timing was out, and he seemed to lack his usual focus and certainty. After a third successive defeat, the coach marched straight up to Gregg. By the look on his face, Gregg knew his patience with him was diminishing. The coach looked him in the eye and said, "This cannot continue. Today's performance was awful, your entire game was pathetic, and I have to seriously consider your future. Play more games like that, and you may be out." He turned and walked away.

Gregg was stunned by this outburst, but then he did something that had a profound effect on his beliefs. For the next day or two, Gregg relentlessly ran the scenario over in his mind. He recalled the words and tone of voice from his coach, and even highlighted the most distressing parts: "You are pathetic, you're awful, you're out." This kept running through his mind like a tape on constant replay. The more he repeated this to himself, the greater the information was fed into his belief programme. He had developed a new belief about his ability and talent that was very different from how it was a few weeks ago.

It's possible for beliefs to be formed quickly with language. Gregg and I worked on changing the words and phrases he had repeated to himself consistently. I explained to him that we all say things in desperation when our plans go wrong. We often throw out comments to motivate people to take drastic action. Unfortunately, we frequently make things much worse, but it's important to remember that his coach's motivation was almost certainly to do anything to regain the quality of performance Gregg had shown in earlier matches.

Gregg changed the phrases he was repeating to himself with phrases that, to him, produced self-belief, desire and confidence. After all, this is what his coach was trying to communicate. He made a list and imagined his coach saying more productive phrases to him with a tone of encouragement. The list of phrases included "You are a class act," "You know how talented you are," "The standards you set are incredibly high," and "I believe you can become world-class." We then introduced a system to change his internal feelings regarding his ability to play at a high level.

Beliefs can be changed with an N.L.P. technique called submodalities. In short, modalities are our five senses. Submodalities are the finer distinctions of each one, and how our mind encodes them.

Here is an example. When you think of your last big win or great performance, notice the pictures in your mind. Firstly, become aware of the position of the picture in your mind's eye. Is it straight in front of you, or off to one side? Perhaps it's large or small. Maybe you see the event through your own eyes, and it fills your entire visual field. You may not have a picture, but a movie. Now, notice any sounds? Are the sounds loud or soft? To the left or the right? Or are there no sounds at all?

All this information is important because you can consciously change this and alter the way you feel. If your picture or movie in your mind is dark and dull, by injecting some vibrant colour, you will create a different response. Mute the sounds or create some, and notice what the effect is. This is easy and great to practice.

Generally, when you see the event through your own eyes and the pictures are bright and colourful, there will be a greater intensity. If you want the feelings to diminish, mute any sounds. Imagine floating up out of your body so you are watching it from a third position (disassociated). If it's a movie, freeze it so it's now a still picture. Drain any colour so it's black and white, and shrink the picture so it's the size of a postage stamp. Finally, imagine the picture either exploding or travelling off into the distance until you can no longer see it.

Do this now and notice the effects. Gregg made alterations to his memory of the event by muting any sounds and freeze-framing the movie of his coach shouting at him. He then drained all the colour so it was black and white. He shrunk the picture so it was the size of a small stamp, and finally imagined it exploding. He practised this until the old negative feelings had weakened considerably.

We were then ready for stage two. He now brought back the picture of his coach; but this time, we designed one where he was looking excited. We made this picture big and bright. I asked him to position it within his visual field until he felt a heightened awareness of positivity. Gregg found that by placing his picture straight in front, it instantly generated a more positive feeling toward his coach; but this positioning can be different for each of us. Next, he changed the still picture to a movie, and finally introduced the new words with a tone of excitement that was both positive and very encouraging.

The result was a very different response concerning his coach. People have commented that the reality is still the same; the coach did all the negative things he remembered. The actuality is that it was his coach's intention which is important. His intention would have been to inject some action and belief into Gregg. What Gregg did was to take the intention and use skills that provided him with the result that all parties wanted.

This exercise is a great one to experiment with. Think of an event that naturally conjures up feelings of anxiety. Drain the colour, shrink the picture, imagine stepping outside your body so you see yourself from a third position, and mute the sounds. Notice how the feelings change. Recreate a new movie, one which inspires you and follows the same steps that Gregg used. Have fun with this.

Techniques used: Modelling, submodalities, choosing a different meaning and language.

Experiences

I received a call from a lady who was a show jumper. She had ridden horses most of her life and, over time, built a passion for competing. A year before, she contacted me. She had suffered a bad fall. She broke her arm and two ribs, and felt a lot of discomfort for several months.

No sooner had she begun her comeback when she suffered another fall. This time, it was much worse. She suffered a broken leg and head injuries. At one point, it was not known if she had suffered any brain damage. For her family, this was agonising.

Fortunately, she made an incredible recovery, and soon wanted to get back into the saddle. Although she had lost none of her confidence to ride, when it came to jumps, she would tense up and almost hold on for dear life. Anyone who rides will know that a horse will sense how the rider feels. When the rider is confident, the horse will respond; but if there's any anxiety, the horse is likely to act in the same way. Her life-threatening experience had created fear, which was increasing every time she attempted to jump. The experience programme was telling her emotional brain that this is a life-threatening act, as the experience had clearly illustrated.

When I watched videos of her before and after her accident, one thing was glaringly obvious. The moment she approached a fence, her physiology changed significantly. In the video of her before the accident, she displayed confidence and authority. Unfortunately, this mindset had departed. She told me how she felt when she was about to jump. She spoke of anguish and distress. Her internal voice would say, "Oh God, just hang on."

The initial task was for her to produce a strong and unwavering physiology, then change the words that she would say to herself. As she would come to the jump, she would now say, "Come on, clear it!" or "Attack this one!" The words would come from the 'sergeant major' inner voice that spoke with a tone of authority.

When she went back to jumping a few weeks later, she had consciously changed both her physiology and internal voice. She was now attacking this head-on, and the results were remarkable. Her experience was a bad one; but by identifying how she had changed, we were able to get her back to her very best and enjoying every moment.

As you already know, one of the prime directives of your emotional brain is to avoid failure. It will fill you with anxiety to extreme levels in the hope that you will sidestep any attempt to take on a task that has a strong possibility of being unsuccessful and, in this case, potentially dangerous. When her experience programme was feeding this information back to her emotional brain, the outcome was inevitable. As you can see, even when a life-threatening incident occurs, it's still within your control to make the appropriate adjustments so there is a calmer response from the emotional brain.

When you compete at any level, you will suffer defeat and endure poor performances. This is not only inevitable, but also vital for long-term success. The reality is that winning is a wonderful feeling, but a very poor teacher. Failure is nearly always seen as something to hide or feel embarrassed about.

Avoiding failure is natural; but from now on, you need to think unnaturally. Take yourself back to the last time you either performed badly, experienced defeat, or both. What was your initial reaction? It's likely you repeated your negative feelings by replaying the performance over and over in your mind. This loads the experience programme with poor data and fuels the response from the emotional brain. You then try to forget about it consciously. Unfortunately, the experience programme can only provide information that is currently stored, and the emotional brain is ready to save you from any more harmful feelings.

You must think about this in a new and invigorating way, and embrace the opportunity to learn. The first question you need to ask yourself after any defeat or poor performance is "How can I make the next performance better?" It's important to ask this question, and NOT "What went wrong?" This will only take you deeper into the negative experience.

I advise you to write down all the ways you can make improvements. List as many as possible; there is no set number. It's important to ask how many. This rightfully implies to your mind that the possibilities for improvements are in abundance. Once you have made your list, decide how many you will include in your next training session or match. I suggest two, but no more than three. Master these improvements before adding the next ones.

This simple change in thinking is what the elite adopt, and you have to fully understand that you must lose and learn before you win at the higher levels. Andy Murray had to suffer Grand Slam final defeats on many occasions. It would be fair to say that the general opinion of many tennis fans was that he would always be second to Federer, Nadal or Djokovic.

Fortunately, Murray firmly understood the vital component of those defeats. He learnt and mastered the missing fragments. On the 5th of November 2016, he became world number one. It's an incredible achievement when you consider the huge challenge of reaching the top in the golden age. It's accepted by many highly respected experts that the men's game was at an unimaginable level.

An athlete who was one of the most committed students I have ever worked with explained to me that he understood how failure could be perceived as an important learning tool; but in his words, "It was simply unacceptable." He told me in no uncertain terms that he could only accept victory. Losing a race was something he couldn't even contemplate.

When I asked how often he worked out in the gym, he proudly said, "Four times every week." I asked him what his goals were while attending the gym. He described how he would push himself to increase the weight or number of reps.

I carried on questioning and asked, "How do you know you have pushed yourself to the limit?"

Without hesitation, he replied, "When I can't do any more. It's the only way I'm going forward and becoming stronger."

I continued, "So you have to fail to get stronger, faster and better?"

A smile appeared on his face. He thought about it, and responded with "Yes, if you like."

By understanding what failure really is, you can use it to reach new heights by creating a positive and committed attitude. When you win, enjoy the elation; if you don't, simply accumulate the learning and drive your progress forward. Think about it... You can only win.

Techniques used: Language, physiology, and failure as learning.

Attitudes

Golf is played and enjoyed by millions worldwide. It's a sport that can be competitive on many levels; but you compete to win, no matter what level you participate in.

The ladies' game is, of course, equally competitive as the men's. I was invited to watch an invitation tournament and discuss some ideas with one of the competitors. She was an experienced player, but she recently found it challenging to make the easy putt on the green. This was infuriating, as her short game was once her strength. She demonstrated what was happening and during those few moments, she became very frustrated and clearly, her physical tension was becoming more intense. She had won this event for the last three years, and was aware that her current form wouldn't be good enough to carry on her winning streak. When we spoke in the clubhouse, she contemplated giving up, which clearly wasn't something she wanted to do.

The day after, we went out on the course to address the problem. Once again, we came to the green, and she rushed her shot and lost any kind of timing. As she played another poor shot, she looked at me and said, "I'm begging the ball to go in so I can get this out of the way." This was significant because her attitude was what we call "going away from". In other words, she was trying to get away from the problem.

What she had to do was to go toward the solution. Her mind was filled with all the possibilities of failure, so I asked her to create a movie in her mind where she was playing her short game with the precision she used to display with consistency. I asked her to make the pictures in her mind big, bright and colourful; and to include any important sounds, see the whole event through her own eyes, and feel the club effortlessly pushing the ball. She would then imagine this before she went to sleep and allow her mind to absorb this information.

The session began in the same way as every session, which is to produce a strong posture. She stood tall and proud, shoulders back with her head held high. I set up a practise routine where I placed several tees on the green. The tasks were to strike the ball and knock the tees over. Once she was playing this with greater consistency, I took the tees away and she focused on her putting. The result was the hole now looks huge, and putting becomes a much easier proposition.

I then moved her attention to the challenge of rushing each shot. In her mind, she was already thinking about how she would play the next shot, or very often reliving the last one that went so badly wrong. Every player understands the importance of being in the moment. Our minds instinctively wonder and contemplate problems we may or may have faced. By being in the present, we automatically clear those unwanted thoughts so our focus is on the job in hand. Our emotional brain is likely to get agitated when things go wrong, so it's important to understand that when we feel these unwanted feelings, it's the emotional brain doing all the thinking. Her challenge was to calm it down.

She accomplished this by learning how to be in the present moment. In the past, she would allow her emotions to take over. This was evident as she played a badly-timed shot out of frustration. Her new plan was to end the habit of reacting to how she felt by stopping for a few seconds, then asking herself, "What's the correct shot that I would play if I had no emotions, and I was simply programmed to play each shot I'm faced with?" I then suggested that every time she played any shot, she would see it as the only shot she would play all day. This wasn't a game of 18 holes, or even 70-plus shots. This was now a game of one shot being played many times.

There have been many occasions where this change in focus has changed a poor mindset that has lingered for years to one of focus and composure. After a short period of time, her attitude had changed from getting away from the problem to going toward the solution. She was no longer fearful of failure, but driving toward success. Like so many techniques, this is simple and directs your focus to the desired outcome.

For a greater understanding of "being in the moment", follow these instructions to achieve the very best result. A good practise routine is to find somewhere quiet with no disturbances. Initially become aware of your breathing. Notice if it's shallow or deep, fast or slow. Don't be tempted to change it; simply become aware of it.

As you continue this routine, it's likely that thoughts will enter your awareness. This is the challenging part. DO NOT fight them in any way. Acknowledge them by taking notice and allowing them to pass. If you fight them, they will persist. I'm sure you have sat in a coffee shop in a busy shopping centre; and as you sit and watch people go by, you may see something that grabs your attention. Perhaps you unexpectedly saw a celebrity, observed your dream car, or witnessed a minor dispute between two or more people. You could walk over and give your opinion; but the most likely result is that you will remain seated, carry on enjoying your coffee, and allow it to pass by. This process is very similar. Allow your thoughts to float by and return your focus to your breathing. With consistent practice, this becomes much easier.

This exercise will produce better focus by excluding outside interference. Focus is a psychological muscle that builds in the same way as a physical muscle. The more you work it, the stronger it gets. Having a clear focus on the present moment helps prevent past experiences and potential future problems from entering your awareness. The results will give you a considerable advantage when you need it the most.

A second practise skill is to read a book whilst listening to some music through a pair of headphones. This is challenging, to say the least, but it strengthens your focus muscle like nothing else.

When someone explains to me that he or she has lost his or her confidence, I first ask, "What is happening?" They will generally explain that they feel negative about their ability to perform and almost expect a poor result. This, of course, is very true; that's precisely how we all feel when it seems that our confidence has been lost. The reality is that we never lose confidence; we do, however, change our focus. When you are struggling, it's almost certain that you will think about the possibilities of something going wrong. A rushed shot, tightness in your body, or a loss in your timing are all experiences you have when you think you have lost confidence. When you are performing well, you tend to only think about and expect to play each shot with a strong mind and a relaxed body.

All these scenarios are a change in focus. Direct your focus to how you want to feel. Where you want to pass the ball or when you will increase your speed are examples of where you must place your thoughts. Being very specific also helps. A tennis player who picks an exact spot for the ball to land when serving is targeting their focus onto what they want. A rugby player can also imagine a spectator sitting in the stands, exactly between the two posts, and holding a bottle of water. When he kicks a penalty, his thoughts are for the ball to physically knock the bottle out of the spectator's hands. By targeting your focus to such high levels of specificity, you place 100% of your attention on what you want. There simply isn't any room for negativity to play any part.

A good phrase to remember is that energy flows where focus goes. Using your 'sergeant major' inner voice will cement your conviction and drown out any timid voice of worry. Always remember to display a strong physiology, and everything changes. By practising these drills, you will find that you can generate much greater levels of confidence simply by redirecting your focus to an outcome you desire.

Techniques used: Moving toward specificity, greater focus, 'sergeant major' inner voice, strong physiology, and mental rehearsal.

Decisions

Your football team are playing in the semi-final of a Cup match. The score is 0-0, the tension is unbearable, and the entire team is terrified of making a mistake. It's the final minute of the game, and your teammate skips past the defender with a clear shot at the goal. He is on the brink of taking the shot when he is pulled back by a defender and misses the ball. The referee has no hesitation in giving your team a penalty. The opposition is demoralised.

Your teammates run over to you with looks of expectation because you're the penalty-taker. In training, you enjoy placing the ball and looking at the fear on the face of the goalkeeper. But this isn't training; this is a one-time opportunity.

However, you change your mind as you look at the goalkeeper while positioning the ball on the spot you're going to shoot it from. You turn away from the goal to take a run-up; but as you turn to face the ball, you change your mind for a second time. This is generating a great deal of anxiety. Instead of taking a few seconds to make a final and definite decision, you run up to take the kick with three options in your mind. The result is a poor kick that is saved by the goalkeeper. You collapse in despair while the goalkeeper is God.

The decision (or lack of it) haunts you; and every time you take a penalty in training, your thoughts seem to remind you that training is very different from a competitive match.

When you do have the opportunity to take a penalty, doubts appear. So, you allow a teammate to take responsibility, with the possibility of him becoming the new hero. All of this is based on one decision.

This is a true story that could have prevented a young and talented player from accomplishing a career in professional football. This one decision was so deep, he felt it impossible to take another penalty in the fear that he would let his team down and experience those terrible emotions again.

When I asked him what was great about that penalty miss, he looked at me with disgust. He leaned forward and said, "Absolutely nothing. It was the worst day of my life!"

I allowed him a few seconds, then asked again. "What was great about that penalty miss?" Before he could conjure up any more negativity, I opened my laptop to reveal a video of England playing West Germany in the World Cup semi-final in 1990. The game finished 1-1, and penalties would decide who went through to the final. Stuart Pearce was one of England's penalty takers. He nervously placed the ball on the spot. He walked away from the ball, ran up apprehensively, kicked it, but the keeper saved. West Germany went on to win the match —and the World Cup. For most, that decision to take a penalty kick in such a huge match would have been their last. But thankfully, Stuart Pearce was not one to allow this decision to define his future.

Fast forward to the 1996 UEFA European Championship. Again, England faced a united Germany in the semi-final. History repeated itself, and the game ended all square: penalty kicks would decide who made it to the final. Once again, Stuart Pearce took responsibility. Marching to the penalty area, he was an unstoppable powerhouse. Placing the ball on the spot, he stepped back, ran up and kicked the ball with force and accuracy. He scored, looked up to the crowd, and displayed not only his commitment to his country, but his unwavering determination to put the record straight.

Stuart Pearce's decision to take the kick in 1990 was not successful. But instead of creating a mindset filled with negativity, he consciously decided that kick would provide the drive to take another equally important one when the day came.

When you look for a different meaning in a decision, you can create a different mindset. When the young player thought about his decision to take the penalty as the biggest learning of his career, he produced a new strategy. He now models himself on Stuart Pearce by taking on a strong physiology; each stride to the penalty box is one of unquestionable supremacy. As he places the ball, he does so with conviction. He instantly picks an exact spot where he will shoot. If he experiences any anxiety, he instantly brings on his personal sergeant major, who says, "Nerves? I don't have time for nerves. Get out of my face. I only have time to smash this into the top corner!"

He then continues his physiology of confidence. He doesn't just run up to the ball; he attacks it with conviction. He understands that he is fully in charge of his thinking and his actions. If the goalkeeper saves it, he can use this experience for greater improvement, with the knowledge that he didn't waver. If he scores, he achieves the desired result. Either way, he always wins. Adopting this state, he places all his energy and focus on the job at hand and greatly increases his chances of scoring.

The decision and experience programmes may seem the same. However, there is one crucial difference. The experience is generally one that happened outside of your control; the decision is something that you consciously decide to do. It's not that important to differentiate between them, but it does explain why they are separate.

Techniques used: Choosing a different meaning, language ('sergeant major' inner voice), physiology and specificity.

Mental Rehearsal

Although we have touched on mental rehearsal, I believe it deserves a dedicated chapter. In the past, some students have not been particularly enthusiastic to learn this. However, when they have experienced the benefits, it becomes one of their routines they always make time for. My advice is to go all-in so you can experience the new you.

How often have you sat, closed your eyes, and imagined playing in a Grand Slam, a World Cup, or an Olympic final? Perhaps you envisaged a dramatic scene where you competed with a ferocious inner strength and composure. The roar of the crowd was deafening, the atmosphere was electric, and you remained focused with a supreme self-belief that will always be remembered.

This is something that feels quite natural when you are very young. In fact, it's an activity that most have played out in their minds as a child. Unfortunately, as we get older, we experience failure without any strategies in place to remain focused. Our programmes are filled up over the years with false data that implies our dreams are simply pictures in our mind and far from reality. This is reinforced by the misguided views of people who we are close to. By the time we know it, we have a belief programme with contents that are driving us away from our ambitions. The emotional brain accepts this data and protects us from any possible failure, and we settle for a fraction of what we are capable of.

I invite you to once again become child-like and forget reality. Reality is based on your past, not your future. Your future is your responsibility, so close the old book of reasons and excuses and begin a journey that could lead you anywhere. You were not born to play it safe. The chances of you even being alive is beyond comprehension, and the fact that you are reading this book suggests that you live in a society where you have ample opportunities.

You now understand failure and how it can propel you forward, and you have a greater knowledge of the overprotective emotional brain and the programmes that can so often mislead it. It's time to roll up your sleeves and push all the "Why I can't do it" and "I'm not that kind of person" excuses to bed for good.

I'm going to explain one of the easiest yet dynamic skills you can learn. You have experienced this when you were younger, but now you will learn how to master it.

It's an incredible fact that your brain cannot tell the difference between something that has happened and something you vividly imagined. This is vital to fully comprehend. The brain creates the same connections in the same way if you imagine performing consistently well or if you physically perform well. Your mind is extremely powerful, but it's likely you take it for granted and rarely use more than a fraction of the inner power that you process.

My challenge for you is simple. Invest time in your schedule to practice this exercise. It will feel awkward, to begin with; and you will naturally tell yourself that you don't have the time. But we all have twenty-four hours in a day. It's up to you how you spend them. So for twenty minutes, three times a week, invest time to practice.

You are about to delve into the world of mental rehearsal. I am sure you have heard of or even tried visualisation. This can be very effective; but during your everyday life, you use more than one sense. It's important to create a mental representation that includes multiple senses. You will use your visual, kinaesthetic, and aural senses. This will build connections in your brain that, with consistent practice, will load new data into your programmes. Now let's begin.

Write down an experience that you could only dream of. This is the time to be bold and not realistic. Remember, reality is based on your past; your focus is now entirely on your future. Take time to conjure up all the possibilities that excite you the most. Your list could include a personal best, a hole-in-one, a maximum break in snooker, scoring a thirty-yard free kick, or hitting it out of the park. Make it a performance goal; in other words, make it something you execute.

This exercise is about producing habit-forming connections so you can become the greatest version of yourself at a deep level of identity. Write down the exciting experiences; and include how you will feel both physically and psychologically, what you will say to yourself before and during your ultimate experience, how you approach the experience and, of course, how you remain calm and controlled, with an irrefutable focus on your performance. This list should be detailed, so invest quality time in designing your goal or goals.

Find somewhere that you can close out the outside world with little or no noise. Make sure your phone is off, and everyone knows that this is your psychological development time. Have a high-backed chair, and make sure you are sitting comfortably. With your eyes open, take a deep breath in through your nose, hold it for a second, and exhale through your mouth. As you allow the breath to release, gently close your eyes.

For a minute, focus all your attention on your breathing and become aware of your breathing pattern. Notice if your breath is shallow or deep. Is it from the abdominal area, or further toward your chest?

Now, direct your focus to the top of your head. Simply become conscious of this area. Ask yourself, "Is there any temperature that I don't normally think about here? Is this area relaxed? Is there any weight that I can notice?" Allow your conscious awareness to remain mindful about this space for around fifteen seconds.

Continue by moving your awareness further down. This will include your eyes, nose, ears and the adjacent back of your head. Once again, ask the very same questions as before; and continue giving each part of your body the same level of attention, from the top of your head to the soles of your feet.

You may find that you'll become very tired, and you may even fall asleep. With practice, you will have the ability to drift slowly into a semi-conscious state. It's that special place between being awake and asleep. It's beyond space and time. You are now in the perfect place to experience an imagined event that seems so real, your programmes will accept the information and store it in the same way as if the event had really happened. This is a very powerful place to be, and one that few ever experience with conscious intent.

After a consistent period of practice, you will be ready to add the second and most significant part of the exercise. As you enter this state of semi-consciousness, you are ready to reload the data in your programmes and allow ideas and virtual experiences to flow effortlessly. The next step is to relive the dreams and experiences you wrote down earlier. Firstly, observe yourself fulfilling your ultimate experience from a third position. In other words, watch yourself and see the new you performing with control, confidence and focus. Make the movie big, bright and colourful. Include any sounds that are important, and allow the inspiration to build inside you. Enjoy watching yourself perform to the highest standards with raised levels of energy.

The final step is to float inside your body and become the great achiever. See the whole event through your eyes, and feel the external feelings and positive internal emotions. Notice how you effortlessly exclude any external interference and calmly draw your attention to the job at hand. Take note of your relaxed body while your focus is unwavering. How does it feel to balance a relaxed physical state with the actions of conviction? Become inquisitive and learn from the very best version of yourself. This takes time and effort. But in the same way as any skill that changes your life, it's time well spent. The more you practice, the faster you will master it.

The focus exercises you studied earlier will be of significant benefit; and as you become more proficient, you will look forward to this exercise. You are in complete control to create an experience that produces excitement and a strong sense of desire. The most important aspect is to become so engrossed, you'll feel the experience is real. When you achieve this level, you will literally be a different person; and as far as your brain is concerned, you are the controlled, confident and focused competitor you dream of every day.

Summary

You will have noticed that in some cases, the process for loading new data into the programmes uses the same techniques. When you identify an event that has held you back, it's helpful to have an instruction manual to follow for a set of simple solutions. It's also important to understand that you can use all or some of the solutions for each one of the programmes. This is not a strict map that has to be followed by the letter, but rather a guide for you to use as an illustration or to experiment with to discover which techniques work best for you.

One aspect that is essential is to reload any programme is language. By adopting this with your chosen techniques, you are ready to reload your programmes and enjoy a very different response from your emotional brain. When a strong physiology is introduced and practised, the complete system becomes an unconscious habit. You are now the creator of your state.

Putting It All Together

You now have a greater understanding of the once-mysterious world of your emotions or, at least, why they would make an appearance when you least want them. The information you have so far places you in a position where over time, you will have the knowledge to completely change your mentality, which provides you with a substantial advantage over your opposition.

To recap what you have so far and demonstrate the system in action, here is an example. Stacey is a pool player. She is competing in an all-or-nothing money match. The match is a race to 21, with the score at 20-20. The last three matches have resulted in defeat; but significantly, she lost when she had an opportunity to clear the table in the final game to win.

She was told by critics and close friends that these big matches are not only risky, but place too much pressure on her. She has heard this on numerous occasions, even from fellow players whom she has huge respect for. Unfortunately, Stacey has found the trap we have all unknowingly fallen into. She repeated their alarming words in her mind on countless occasions, and she relives their look of concern as well as their tone of despair.

All this information over time has been fed and stored in the programmes; so when she finds herself at the table with an opportunity to finish the match, this is what happens. The match is locked at 20-20 when she is unexpectedly given an opportunity to seal the win. This information enters her awareness, where an interpretation is created by the programmes. The programmes then feed their analysis to the emotional brain.

As you are now aware, it does this to gather any information that may indicate if or how it needs to respond.

The experience programme says, "These situations are why we shouldn't play these big matches." The decision programme says, "I should never put myself forward to play these big games." The belief programme adds, "Players whom I respect have told me with certainty that I don't have what it takes to clear the table under pressure." The language programme then adds all the words that players, family members and critics have given with their tone of dread. The attitude programme begins to speed up the whole thought process in the hope that she can get this out of the way.

All this information is offered to the emotional brain, which will now go into "panic mode" and do anything to prevent her from going through this again. It will fill her mind with negative thoughts; and her body, with nerves and anxiety to whatever level it feels necessary to ensure she puts a stop to this and moves to a safer place, where she will avoid failure and elude any possibility of others seeing her as a loser. In simple terms, the emotional brain demands that she quits. This is an experience that nearly all competitors of any sport have endured.

The Solution

Having a greater understanding of how all this works instantly gives Stacey an advantage. She now knows that her negative thoughts and feelings are the cunning work of her overthinking and primitive emotional brain. Its behaviour is generated entirely to protect her.

By reloading the data in the programmes, the response from the emotional brain will be vastly different. She is now taking a much greater level of control. The more she reloads new data, the closer she comes to being the master of her thinking and emotions.

To assist Stacey in changing the data in her programmes, she has a new thought process. She now consciously takes her focus to aspects she can control. Firstly, she accepts that other people's opinions are based on what they see, not what they know. She brings back the picture in her mind of concerned people whom she respects and cares about, drains the colour, mutes any sounds, and imagines floating out of her own body so that she sees the event as a fly on the wall or from a third position. She then visualises the image exploding before creating a new one.

The replacement image shows the same people now looking excited and happy for her. (That's always been their intention.) The new picture is upgraded to a movie that's big, bright, and colourful; and includes sounds that promote elation and enthusiasm. She remains conscious of her internal voice; and at any suggestion that she is creating the language that could conjure up pictures or movies in her mind where she is struggling to perform, she immediately brings in her sergeant major. He banishes any discouraging words, and replaces them with phrases that promote self-belief and confidence with a tone of certainty. She maintains a physiology that promotes assurance and poise. Each step, every gesture is one of conviction.

She has looked at previous defeats and listed all the ways she can implement new ideas that produce a better all-around performance. Stacey's schedule includes a list of performance goals which she mentally rehearses three times a week. Her all-time hero is the winner of 50 professional pool titles, Allison Fisher. She invests at least thirty minutes a day watching and listening to Allison on any media that's available. During these precious moments, she makes sure everyone knows this is important psychological development time. She sits with her headphones on and becomes enthralled in the world of one of the greats. Over time, this will collectively load the programmes with quality data.

One other (and very important) alteration is a change of focus. To help her place her attention solely on her performance, she plays every shot as if it's the only shot she will play all day. To assist with the high level of focus, Stacey has implemented a simple four-step strategy, which looks like this. As soon as she decides the shot, she will play it; she refuses to deviate. She then decides the exact spot where the white ball will come to rest. As she plays the shot, her intention is for the object ball to go clean in the pocket. Just going in off the jaws of the pocket is not good enough; it must crack the back of the pocket. She is aware of the precise position the white ball must land on as she accelerates the cue through it. Finally, she remains completely still on the shot and remains in this position for a few seconds after. As soon as she completes the shot, she takes the next one with the same thought process. Remember, precision is a great way to produce a laser focus as including a simple strategy will increase it to an even higher level.

The long-term results are significant. Before Stacey goes to sleep, she runs through the four-step process in her mind. She makes sure she includes not only the visual part, but also the feelings of her perfect cue action, the sounds of the balls cracking the back of the pocket, and the applause from enthusiastic spectators.

Stacey's Four-Step Strategy

1. In a practice environment, Stacey would see the correct shot to play very quickly. She would never hesitate, so the strategy is to see the shot and go "all-in". She refuses to deviate from that instinctive decision.

2. She picks the exact position she wants the cue ball to land. Again, she is taking her focus to a specific spot.

3. As she plays the shot, her intention is for the ball to go in cleanly, not rattling in off the jaws. Once again, this creates a laser focus.

4. As she plays the shot, she is aware of the spot the cue ball needs to land on. She then accelerates the cue through the white ball and consciously remains rock-steady. She remains in this position until the object ball is in the pocket.

This is very straightforward, but she is now able to change the data in the programmes leading up to the match, and understand that she has a very simple four-step process to follow during the match. As always, the emphasis is on producing a positive state and directing her focus to the process (actions), and letting the result take care of itself.

Additional Skills

You now have all the skills to reload the data in the programmes. But I want to give you some additional skills. These work with the techniques you have so far. By implementing this section, you will be the complete competitor. Take your time to master what you have already learnt, but we'll begin this section of the book by increasing the pace.

Let's Speed Things Up

As you practice all the skills in this book, a remarkable change will happen. The long-term transformation will come partly from a greater awareness of the emotional brain and how the programmes guide it. You will also gain the knowledge and capability to change the data in the programmes that automatically alter the response from the emotional brain.

However, our modern society has encouraged us to demand instant results. If your computer fails to open a programme within a few seconds, you are likely to question if it's nearing the end of its life, or perhaps a new model will perform at the speed you expect. The fact is that we demand quick results or our interest diminishes rapidly. So, it's important to remind yourself that the time invested in practising these skills will give you a lifetime of self-belief, greater confidence, certainty and control.

I know from experience that having some assistance when you need an instant change will help you remain focused on the complete programme. To help you remain enthusiastic, I have a couple of tricks that will produce a change of state instantly. They will assist in your development and help reload the programmes.

The next two chapters are fast skills. They have been developed to utilise the immense energy of the emotional brain. The first one is called instant self-belief. It allows the emotional brain to start becoming energised, then directs all the energy to precisely where you need it.

Instant Self-Belief
(Stepping Out of the Comfort Zone)

Josh was an enthusiastic and talented tennis player. Although he was new to the game, he quickly found that he had a natural eye-to-ball coordination. Before long, he began playing competitively.

During his first competition, he beat two very accomplished players and was approached by the club's resident coach. He signed up for lessons, which led him to a semi-final appearance just two months later. Josh went on to win his first competition after spending only three months with the coach. He had quickly gained a reputation for being an incredibly fast and agile player.

At the later stages of the summer season, Josh was asked to play for his county. To Josh, this was unsurprising; because of his current form and speed, he advanced from complete beginner to one of the best players at the club. He was enjoying the attention of players, spectators and other coaches. He played his first match for the county and won convincingly.

His second match had much more importance attached to it. This was the decider; and his opponent was an experienced player, although his form was somewhat

79

inconsistent and the view from both sides was that Josh would be the favourite. As expected, Josh began well and opened a lead. He felt comfortable and relaxed when his opponent suddenly rediscovered his form and made an incredible comeback.

Before long, the match was all square. For the first time, Josh's fortitude was called into question. It was his service game, and this was a must-win game to stop the rot and to put himself back into contention. The anguish was apparent on the faces of his teammates and travelling supporters. He made his way to the baseline.

This is where the emotional brain would normally be in full flow: flooding his mind with negative dialogue, severe nerves and, just to make sure he is aware of its presence, he would begin to physically shake. However, I'm going to give you a strategy that Josh applied to utilise the incredible energy from the emotional brain to good use.

Let's look at this scenario with the new strategy in place. Josh is in his seat as the emotional brain begins to engage and respond with fear and trepidation. Initially, Josh closes his eyes and creates an image of traffic lights. He can see the red, amber and green lights. As he looks at the red light, he says to himself with complete certainty: "STOP!" (It's vital that this is said as a command. He is completely changing the direction of his focus. N.L.P. calls this a 'state break'.) He then becomes aware of the amber light and says to himself, in the same tone: "READY!" Finally, his focus is on the green light, and he shouts to himself: "GO!!"

He now opens his eyes and marches to the baseline. He checks his physiology; makes sure he stands tall and proud, with shoulders back and head held high. He walks with poise and certainty. Upon arriving at the line, his focus is solely on the precise spot where he will serve the ball. He then introduces his new inner voice, the sergeant major, who says something like this: "Bounce the ball three times and stand up tall, proud and menacing. Pick the exact point in the service box the ball will fire into. If my opponent gets near it, the ball will take the racket out of his hand." (Remember to avoid picking an area, but select an exact spot. Energy flows where focus goes, so direct it exactly where you want it.) As he prepares to bounce the ball, the sergeant major adds one more command: "Fire it like a bullet so it bounces out the court!"

By using the traffic-light system to produce the change of focus, and combining the physiology of certainty and the 'sergeant major' inner voice, Josh has deployed an assault on his negative feelings and any self-doubt. He is using the energy that is naturally generated and directing it to a state of complete commitment. He has designed the ultimate strategy of self-belief in an instant.

A youth player at a well-known football academy used the same technique when he had a discussion with the coaching staff about playing at a higher level. He felt that he had displayed enough quality to play in the under-21 team. He was naturally an introvert, so this often prevented him from expressing to others his confidence and ambitions. After I explained the instant self-belief technique to him, he enlightened me that he was going to the club's Christmas party, and the coaching staff at all levels would be present.

This is what he did. As soon as he spotted the coach from the youth squad, he knew he had to act quickly before his emotional brain completely took over and filled his mind with doubt. As he felt his nervous energy rise, he closed his eyes and imagined the traffic lights. He went from red, amber and green together with voicing the 'stop, ready and go!' commands with a tone of authority. He then checked his physiology. He walked with purpose toward the coach and activated his sergeant major, which said: "Get over to the coach and make sure he knows you are much more than a youth player. You're good enough to play in the under-21 team and potentially a member of the first team. Shake his hand with conviction and confidence. Just do it; no excuses!"

Now, you may think the story ends with the coach giving the youth player exactly what he wanted, and his dreams becoming reality. But this is what really happened. The coach sat him down and expressed his gratitude that this young player had used his initiative to talk so positively about his future. But he felt that he needed more time at youth level to cement his confidence and continue his education of the game. The player then walked away with the knowledge that although he didn't get the result he had hoped for, he had displayed huge courage and had smashed out of his comfort zone, showing a maturity that the coaching staff had never seen before. His courage was producing an incredible inner strength.

How many times this week have you considered confronting a difficult task; but upon deliberation, decided to back away? Maybe you talked yourself out of it, or an old memory has awoken along with the feelings of disappointment or fear. Here's a rule to remember: If you know it's the right thing to do but it feels incredibly scary, you need to go for it to grow and expand. The path to most resistance is the one you must take before these old feelings take over, so act and attack the fear.

The Steps for Instant Self-Belief (Stepping Out of the Comfort Zone)

1. As soon as you take on a task that's out of your comfort zone, it's likely you will feel nerves increasing.
2. The very moment this happens, close your eyes and imagine the set of traffic lights. This simply means you steer your focus to a completely new direction.
3. Observe the red light and say loudly to yourself, "Stop!" Look at the amber light and voice out, "Get ready!" Finally, notice the green light and shout to yourself, "Go!"
4. Instantly make the physical move with a strong physiology. Every step and every gesture is one of complete conviction.
5. Introduce your sergeant major. His commanding tone needs to be loud, with words of necessity. He demands you remain focused and totally committed. He fills your mind with certainty and conviction, which are non-negotiable.
6. The sergeant major continues alongside your strong physiology so you can begin and complete the task.
7. Whatever the result, you must congratulate yourself, as pushing outside your old boundaries is an act of

courage. If you use this technique to take on a difficult task, you will, in time, change your success to levels you may never have thought possible.

The Rapid-Change Technique

The instant self-belief strategy is a fast and effective way to immediately redirect your focus from fear of and anxiety in a situation to a non-negotiable all-out attack toward your chosen outcome. For the majority, this has the desired effect. But for some, the emotional brain can become so overwhelming, a strategy loaded with more power is required.

Have you ever suffered so badly from nerves that you felt you had a phobia of competition? You reached the point where you may endure panic attacks, and competing becomes terrifying. If you have ever suffered to this degree, you are not alone. This happens to more talented people than you may imagine who suffer in silence, almost embarrassed to share their feelings with others.

A seventeen-year-old golfer came to me in despair. He had, in his own words, tried everything. His coach was losing patience; and he feared he was going to become another player who promised so much, only to fade away. During his early teens, he was dominant in club and county competitions. He quickly became the player everyone knew and feared. Some described him as arrogant, something he strongly denied. He described himself as possessing a cast-iron self-belief (I agreed with his version). As soon as he walked onto the course, he felt he owned it. He never played to simply compete; he always attended every match with the sole intention of destroying the opposition. His long game was outstanding, and his putting was extremely consistent.

From an early age, he had his sights firmly set on becoming one of the very best in the world. Unfortunately, he was (at the time of our meeting) a shadow of his former self. I'm sure this story is one that resonates with many people. But fortunately, in this instance, we designed and implemented a solution. The player was prepared to put his heart and soul into our work together, and I invite you to do the same. He would practise his techniques with the same level of desire and commitment that he demonstrated in the training sessions for the physical side of his game.

Before we began our work, I asked him what had to happen for him to become (in his words) terrified when he was about to play. He described how he would sit in the clubhouse; look out on the course; and automatically envisage a performance that was filled with hesitation, poor timing, a lack of commitment, and an absence of any self-belief. His body would fill with anxiety; and, on one occasion, was physically sick.

This movie had become so powerful that we had to tone it down considerably. I tasked him to recreate the movie in his mind, but make some alterations. Firstly, he imagined stepping out of his body, so he is in the third position. The movie was bright and colourful, so my instruction was to drain the colour away so it became black and white. He paused the movie to convert it into a still picture. He then shrunk

87

the picture so it was now the size of a postage stamp. Any sounds that were relevant were muted. Finally, he allowed the picture to explode into an infinite number of pieces.

He practised this for a couple of days, although he noticed changes instantly. For many people, this alone has the potential to extract the nervous energy. But in this instance, more work was required.

The second part of the exercise was crucial. We started by designing the most incredible scenario. It had to include three important characteristics: visuals, audio and kinaesthesia. In other words, he produced a new movie in his mind that was visual with sounds and feelings. We took some time creating this, ensuring it instantly generated excitement. His new movie was of him teeing off; feeling a relaxed, powerful and effortless swing; hearing the sweet sound of the perfectly struck ball; and watching it (seeing the event through his own eyes) launch with laser precision, pace and power. The new movie was big, bright and colourful. The sounds were exciting and loud. The positive feelings that developed when he watched it in his mind were getting stronger every day.

I pointed out a fact that took some time to sink in. The physical feelings of heightened anxiety are generally a faster heart rate, butterflies in the stomach, and tension in the body. When you feel intense excitement, you are likely to experience a faster heart rate, butterflies in the stomach, and tension in the body. This is extremely important to understand. The physical feelings of anxiety are the same as the feelings of intense excitement. By accepting this, we can trick the emotional brain and use its huge volume of energy to drive us forward.

He was now ready to put his new plan into operation. As soon as he felt the feelings of anxiety, he would deploy his new tactic. Initially, with his eyes closed, he would visualise a set of traffic lights and say the commands associated with the three colours. (Remember, this changes the direction of focus.) This was his trigger to introduce the new movie he had rehearsed that included the feelings of his relaxed, powerful swing; the sound of the club connecting with the ball; and the sight of the ball launching high in the air with laser precision.

As soon as he activated the new movie, he then deployed his sergeant major, who said in a commanding tone, "I've never felt so excited. I feel incredible!" His emotional brain would link the exciting movie to his physical feelings, accept that they were a match, and allow things to continue. He now checked his physiology. He was excited, confident, self-assured, and ready to become the dominant force.

Possibly the most important aspect of this new strategy was that it put him in control of his emotions when he once felt so vulnerable. During the following days and weeks, he was likely to face situations that would normally trigger extreme anxiety. During these testing times, he would consistently practice his new skill. In the first few attempts, the positive effect lasted a few minutes. However, the more he rehearsed it, the more proficient he became. By practising this skill along with all the others we have covered in the book (so far), he has now built an automatic response to difficult situations. All his programmes are positively changing. He uses this model not only in sport, but anytime he is challenged by situations that would normally provoke old feelings of extreme anxiety.

Another example of the technique in action occurred when a pool player had a winner-takes-all match for a considerable sum of money. His major challenge was controlling his nerves during the first few games. The match was a race to 21, so a good start is imperative. As he walked into the venue, he would feel the strong physical feelings of anxiety (which again included a faster heart rate, butterflies in his stomach, and tension in the body). We sat and wrote down what would have to happen for him to feel confident and self-assured. The conclusion was for him to pot the last few balls with a relaxed body and a totally focused mind.

Once again, we had to include three components: visuals, kinaesthesia, and audio. His new movie was him potting the last few balls to win the match. His body was relaxed, and the feeling of his cue accelerating through the ball was perfection. The sounds of the audience applauding his final few shots automatically made him smile, and he imagined watching the balls crack the back of the pocket. This new movie generated excitement, confidence, and feelings of total self-belief. The task was to deploy this when required.

The evening of the match arrived. He walked into the arena and opened his cue case, which initiated his anxiety. He stood by his seat, closed his eyes, and visualised the traffic lights and their commands: stop, get ready, go. He then launched the new movie. He made the pictures big and bright, the sounds loud, and the feelings as intense as possible. As the movie played, he used his 'sergeant major' commanding tone and said to himself, "I've never felt so excited. I feel incredible!" His emotional brain linked the new movie to the physical feelings, accepted that they are a match, and allowed the excitement to continue. Finally, as always, he checked his physiology. Again, he had to repeat this a few times during the first few games, but the desired effect was accomplished.

The Steps for the Rapid-Change Technique

1. Become aware of situations when you are likely to feel extremely anxious.

2. Remember that the physical feelings of anxiety and nerves are a faster heart rate, butterflies in the stomach, and tension in the body. The physical feelings of excitement are the same.

3. Create a movie in your mind that portrays a successful completion of the challenge that triggered the anxiety.

4. The new movie must include exciting pictures, feelings and sounds.

5. As soon as the old anxiety commences, close your eyes and imagine the traffic lights. Observe the red light and say to yourself, "Stop!" Look at the amber light and say, "Get ready!" Finally, notice the green light and shout to yourself, "Go!"

6. Run the new movie in your mind.

7. Using the 'sergeant major' commanding tone, voice loudly to yourself, "I've never felt so excited. I feel incredible!"

8. The emotional brain links the exciting movie to the physical feelings, accepts that they match, and allows it to continue.

9. Check your physiology and ensure that it's one of authority.

10. It's highly likely you will have to repeat this a few times. However, the more you do it, the longer it lasts, and the faster it initiates.

11. Have fun.

At this point, you can be forgiven for thinking you only need the fast skills. After all, they immediately direct your focus and attention to the perfect competitive state. So why do you need all the information offered? Reloading the programmes over time results in an automatic response from the emotional brain. When all the programmes have been reloaded with data that work for you, situations that were once perceived challenging will automatically feel more comfortable, with higher energy levels and a clear mind. This will take place without conscious effort. It essentially becomes a habit.

Simply relying on fast skills will have a positive effect, as demonstrated, but always relies on you activating them. Programme data-changing has a long-term effect by implementing the complete system, significantly reducing the need to use "fast skills", but they do provide a fast response when testing difficult or potentially terrifying situations. Work with the entire programme and over time, you not only become a different competitor, but a different person.

Goal Setting

If you are about to embark on a journey, it's a good idea to know how you are going to reach your destination. This may seem glaringly obvious; but every hour of every day, people are investing their precious time working hard on their sport, sacrificing nights out and weekends away in the hope of achieving their full potential. For some, it's completing a marathon, whilst others have ambitions of competing for their county or country. We all have individual ambitions. However, I have witnessed on countless occasions dedicated people who have no idea of how they will accomplish it. They seem to have a misguided view that if they keep training, everything will naturally fall into place. Unfortunately, this is simply not the case. It's essential to have a plan of action or a strategy set up so that you can monitor your progress and remain on course.

Goal setting is often misunderstood and completely undervalued by players and coaches. If I ask someone "Why are you training" or "What are you training for", I learn about their short-term and long-term ambitions. If I ask what their detailed plans are or how they plan to reach those ambitions, far too often I'm faced with a look of uncertainty.

One of the biggest mistakes people make is to write down their big goal and stop there. They look at their dream in written form day and night in the hope that it will somehow develop into reality. Now, writing your goals down is vital. It means you are serious about them. However, as you now know, the emotional brain is made in part to protect you from any possible failure. If you simply write down a goal that hinges on winning an event, the emotional brain, with the help of the programmes, is likely to become anxious if it feels you are setting an ambitious target, especially if it's not entirely within your control. At this point, it's important to understand that I would never tell anyone they can't win World, Olympic, National or Club titles. However, there is a better way to give yourself the opportunity to reach these heights whilst managing the reactions of your emotional brain.

Goal setting is for anyone of any ability; but no matter who you are, you must begin with the desired destination. Let's say the goal is to run a marathon. Whatever your goal is, take a moment to work out and write down your "Why". The "Why" is the purpose for doing it. For example, the purpose of running a marathon could be that you believe it's an incredible feat for any human being. Maybe you were once overweight and extremely unfit; running those 26 miles is the moment you celebrate a huge transformation in your health and wellbeing. Or maybe you are running for a charity that is close to your heart. Whatever it is, make sure your reasons for doing it are strong. This will be vital when the training gets tough. It's also important to include the time frame in which you want to achieve it.

Now, direct and produce a movie in your mind. This includes what you will see and hear, and how you will feel. If your goal is to run a marathon, it would include how the final mile will look like as the crowd claps with unlimited enthusiasm. Your feelings will be of confidence coupled with self-belief and purpose. As always, make it big, bright and full of colour. Turn up the volume on the sounds and feelings. This will produce a burning desire and a hunger to accomplish your ambition. Let's assume the time frame to achieve the goal is one year.

The second step is to reverse engineer the goal. This is accomplished by simply positioning the achieved goal at month 12 and working all the way back to the present moment with monthly goals. These smaller goals are performance goals. These are the performance standards you set for yourself that build towards your big goal. For completing a marathon, these include distance, speed training and psychological preparation. So, the plan may look something like this:

Month 1: Walk 20 mins three times a week.

Month 2: Walk 30 mins three times a week.

Month 3: Walk 15 mins, followed by a 15-min slow jog.

Month 4: Jog three times a week for four to five miles.

Month 5: Jog three times a week for five to seven miles.

Month 6: Jog three times a week for seven to nine miles.

Month 7: Jog seven miles at a medium pace.

Month 8: Jog nine miles at a slow pace.

Month 9: Jog twelve miles at a slow pace.

Month 10: Jog nine miles at a medium pace.

Month 11: Jog twelve miles at a slow pace.

Month 12: Jog nineteen miles at a slow pace.

Now you're ready to enjoy the magical day.

I would also encourage you to join the Facebook group "Sports Psychology Made Easy" (https://www.facebook.com/groups/436463539726916/). Incorporate a nutritional programme with daily portions, and ensure you have a consistent sleep pattern.

This is in no way a complete plan for a marathon runner. In fact, you will need to set up weekly and daily goals. But it gives you an idea of how goal setting works. Look at your written "why" and mentally relive your big goal every Sunday evening. This is a reminder of the importance of the goal, and to recreate the passion and excitement.

After you have relived your future experience, examine your tasks for the coming week. Take a few minutes to remind yourself of your schedule for the coming seven days. Each day of the week focuses solely on the mission for that day. Remember, the most important aspect is that you remain focused on the standard you need to reach each day as opposed to the end result.

As the circle for success explains, when we put our attention on our state and actions, the results will take care of themselves. The most common mistake is to repeat the gruelling 26-mile challenge in your mind both night and day. By running this thought over and over, you are likely to lose motivation, and place your focus on its difficulty. By placing your attention on the daily task, you can celebrate simple triumphs regularly. In fact, ensure you congratulate yourself for your achievements every time you accomplish them; this is vital.

As you now know, the way we communicate with ourselves has a huge impact on our programmes, emotional brain, state, and long-term success. So be mindful of the words you use on yourself and the tone in which you deliver it. Use your sergeant major to keep you focused and prevent negative self-talk. Always be aware of your physiology; and remember, all of this is nothing more than a decision you make every day. So, make a promise to yourself that you will follow the plan. Commit to it by having a clear focus on the day's goals that you are responsible for. Even though it's tempting, never look at the following day's agenda. Make all these your obligation, your duty with no compromise. You will be astonished at the results.

Relaxed Body

Throughout the book, we have looked at ways to produce the ultimate state of mind. When you study, and most importantly, put all your knowledge into practice, with consistency you will become a very different competitor.

During feedback sessions, I always encourage people to inform me of any challenges they face. One comes up more than any other. During the early days of learning these new skills, your focus will be on the mind, so the body can become tense and inflexible. Obviously, this is likely to prevent good timing when striking a ball or getting the right flow when running. I have two solutions; try both and decide which feels more natural to you and works for you while you're competing.

Progressive Relaxation

The name says it all, and it's a very easy skill to learn. One of its main advantages is that it can be used without your opponent or spectators noticing. It can be performed in a matter of seconds; so for tennis players, athletes or footballers, this is a great one to learn.

Take a deep breath in and tense the muscles in your body. Hold this for just a couple of seconds. Firstly, release approximately a third of the tension and the breath you are holding. After a second or two, release another third before breathing out fully and allowing all the tension to drain away.

It can help if you say words to yourself that describe the desired result. "Relax", "release" or "let go" can all help to achieve the very best outcome. If you often feel tense but find it difficult to release, then this may be the exercise you have been looking for. Invest time to practice this.

Some of my students found it helpful to begin by focusing on different parts of their body. For example, they worked on their upper body, shoulders, arms and neck. The following day, they worked on their chest, stomach and back. The more you practise, the more natural it becomes.

One word of warning. If you have suffered any broken bones, pulled a muscle, or had any kind of injury, consult a doctor first. If you are advised to leave this exercise, then the following one will be just as effective.

The Red Mist

As we have discovered, the mind, as clever as it is, cannot differentiate between what's vividly imagined and what's real. Your mind loves metaphors; after all, you were brought up with it.

When you were very young, parents, carers and teachers told stories to promote values and beliefs in the hope that one day, you will become a caring and well-behaved adult. Storytelling continues to influence beliefs all through your life, and none more than television and film. How often have you watched a drama or a movie simply because you liked the actors and actresses? A few minutes into the plot, you find yourself having an emotional attachment to the character, not the person acting. This is natural, and you can use this to your advantage for the next skill set.

The Red Mist is also a metaphor that has helped a countless number of athletes physically relax. I will explain how this worked for a golfer who suffered from high levels of tension in his upper body before playing a shot. First, he would identify the location of the tension, and imagine that area was the colour red. He would visualise the red area transforming into a red mist before taking a deep breath in through his nose, and imagining the red mist being vacuumed and settling on an internal shelf just above his chest. Finally, through his mouth, he would exhale and once again use his imagination to visualise the red mist leaving his body. He then scanned the area to check that all the tension was released. If there was still evidence of it, he simply repeated the process. With practice, he rarely needed more than one exhalation.

For the majority, this is enough. But if you want to feel greater levels of relaxation, then a blue mist can be added. Take another deep breath in; but this time, imagine inhaling a blue mist. This is the colour of relaxation. Become aware of the blue mist effortlessly travelling to the area in the body where relaxation is required. Take a few moments to allow this sensation to settle. The more you use this technique, the faster your mind and body will react.

For some, like all other skills, this feels very natural and the results will occur without too much effort. For the majority, it will take a concentrated effort. To have a mind that has a clear focus and a burning desire coupled with a body that's flexible and stress-free is the perfect combination. You can produce this no matter what the occasion or the situation.

It's All Yours

It's worth remembering that consistent effort will be required to overcome feelings of frustration, anxiety or fear. Every sportsperson must continually go outside their comfort zone and experience the psychological challenges that must be faced so that they can grow.

Most will make a few attempts, and then allow their emotional brain to flood their minds with reasons and excuses that give them a way out. Do not let this be you. For you to grow, you must adopt a new attitude. If you remain with the old one, then it will be reasonable to accept that nothing will change.

Embrace the new you, and look forward to pushing yourself and appreciating your progress. You now have all the skills you need to produce a mindset wherein you can approach any situation with complete control of your thinking. When you go into an event 100% confident that you will give everything, you go into the event with 100% confidence. You are leaving situations behind that are out of your control; and by placing your focus on the performance, you greatly increase your chances for the desired result.

My motivation for writing this book is to have a positive effect on as many people as humanly possible. As a competitor, you will spend a great deal of time working on your game. Sacrifices must be made: while your friends meet up for a night out, your priority is to turn up for training; and for many, push their bodies to extreme levels. All of this happens so you can enjoy the feelings of intense excitement and elation that few can ever imagine.

We all have the same number of hours in our day, and we choose how to use them. Every-one of us find it natural to move toward comfort and ease, but taking this path will never take you to the destination of success and achievement. Always take the path to most resistance; this alone will separate you from the clear majority.

Each day you wake up, decide that you will attack the day. When the alarm goes off, step into the winner's shoes, make the move without delay, and walk with physiology of certainty. Use the 'sergeant major' internal voice to create a focus that drives you to what you want. Use words of necessity and a tone of conviction. This is a daily routine because to keep your success alive, you must attend to it every day. When you enter the training arena, always give everything. When I say everything, I mean 100%.

Here is a thought that you should write down and put somewhere that you can see before you leave home. If you are only willing to give 99%, then you are going 1% back. This may sound heartless and unforgiving, but putting in 100% will give you the very best results you are capable of.

My goal is for you to fulfil your true potential, not the potential that others think you can achieve. Together, we must ensure you have a group of strategies that upgrade your thinking. When you have control over your thoughts, you will produce very different emotions and actions which, in time, naturally yield much better results. No more excuses; roll up your sleeves and take 100% responsibility. Destroy your demons and anxieties, and create confidence with an unlimited self-belief. It's time to start winning.

Printed in Great Britain
by Amazon